MW01532962

welcome

These quotations were gathered lovingly but unscientifically over several years and/or contributed by many friends or acquaintances. Some arrived, and survived in our files, on scraps of paper and may therefore be imperfectly worded or attributed. To the authors, contributors and original sources, our thanks, and where appropriate, our apologies.—The editors

CREDITS

Compiled by Dan Zadra
Designed by Steve Potter

ISBN: 1-932319-38-7

Printed in China

Practice hospitality.

ROMANS 12:13

HOSPITALITY MEANS WE TAKE
PEOPLE INTO OUR LIVES, MINDS,
HEARTS, WORK AND EFFORTS.

JOAN D. CHITTISTER

Come at evening

or at morning.

Come when expected

or without warning.

A thousand welcomes

you'll find here before you.

And the oftener you come,

the more we'll

adore you.

WELCOME SIGN, 1870

A FEELING OF
HOME
IN THE WORLD
COMES THROUGH
CARING AND
BEING CARED FOR.

MILTON MAYEROFF

Come! Let us heap

up the fire and

sit hunched by the

flame together, and

make a friend of it.

HUMBERT WOLFE

Beauty is everywhere a welcome guest.

GOETHE

I have never been a millionaire. But I have enjoyed a warm welcome, a great meal, a crackling fire, and a glorious sunset. There are plenty of life's tiny delights for all of us.

JACK ANTHONY

With her whole heart's
welcome in her smile.

CAROLINE NORTON

YOURS WAS ONLY A SUNNY SMILE,

BUT IT SCATTERED THE NIGHT

AND LITTLE IT COST IN THE GIVING—

LIKE MORNING LIGHT,

AND MADE THE DAY WORTH LIVING.

UNKNOWN

LESS ROUTINE
AND MORE LIFE.

AMOS ALCOTT

In between goals
is a thing
called life,
that has to
be lived
and enjoyed.

SID CAESAR

LET'S SPEND

THE AFTERNOON.

WE CAN'T TAKE IT

WITH US.

ANNIE DILLARD

Life is ours to be spent, not saved.

D.H. LAWRENCE

JOY ENTERS THE ROOM. IT SETTLES ON THE WINDOWSILL, WAITING TO SEE WHETHER IT WILL BE WELCOME HERE.

KIM CHERNIN

The place to be happy
is here.
The time to be happy
is now.
The way to be happy
is to make others so.

ROBERT G. INGERSOLL

IT IS A GREAT ART TO SAUNTER.

HENRY DAVID THOREAU

SO COME, AND SLOWLY
WE WILL WALK
THROUGH GREEN
GARDENS AND
MARVEL
AT THIS STRANGE
AND SWEET WORLD.

SYLVIA PLATH

THE MOST PRECIOUS
THINGS OF LIFE
ARE NEAR AT HAND.

JOHN BURROUGHS

Hold out your hands

to feel the luxury

of the sunbeams.

HELEN KELLER

The main thing

is that we

hear and enjoy

life's music

everywhere.

THEODORE FONTANE

I enjoy early mornings on the porch; fresh corn; going barefoot; blueberries and strawberries and raspberries; sleeping without night-clothes or covers; the long evenings and the texture of the low western sun on fields that are still green.

DONALD M. MURRAY

There is no stress in the world.

EARL HIPP

TENSION IS WHO WE
THINK WE SHOULD BE.
RELAXATION IS
WHO WE ARE.

PROVERB

Ah!
To do
nothing—
and
to do
it well.

VERONIQUE VIENNE

The work will
wait while you
show the child
the rainbow, but
the rainbow won't
wait while you
finish the work.

PAT CLAFFORD

I WISH YOU ALL THE JOY
THAT YOU CAN WISH.

WILLIAM SHAKESPEARE

I'd like to
brush the gray
from out of
your skies
and leave them
only blue.

EDGAR GUEST

SERVICE IS NOTHING BUT LOVE IN WORK CLOTHES.

UNKNOWN

AFTER THE VERB "TO LOVE"...
"TO HELP" IS THE MOST
BEAUTIFUL VERB
IN THE WORLD.

BERTHA VON SUTTNER

LAUGHTER
IS ALWAYS BRIGHTEST
WHERE THE
FOOD
IS THE BEST.

IRISH PROVERB

No matter where
I take my guests,
it seems they like
my kitchen best.

PENNSYLVANIA DUTCH SAYING

STRANGERS ARE FRIENDS WE HAVE YET TO MEET.

JIM HATHAWAY

For memory has painted this perfect day with colors that never fade, and we find at the end of a perfect day the soul of a friend we've made.

CARRIE JACOBS BOND

WHEN YOU'RE TRAVELING,

YOU ARE WHAT YOU ARE,

RIGHT THERE AND THEN.

PEOPLE DON'T HAVE YOUR

PAST TO HOLD AGAINST YOU.

NO YESTERDAYS ON THE ROAD.

WILLIAM LEAST HEAT-MOON

Wisdom comes
not from
the miles we travel
along life's journey,
but from
the stops we make,
the people we meet,
and the hearts
we're willing
to hear.

LARRY DOBBS

Take time

to enjoy

other hearts

to your

heart's content.

UNKNOWN

The cream of enjoyment in this life is always impromptu: The chance walk; the unexpected visit;the unpremeditated journey; the unsought conversation or acquaintance.

FANNY FERN

NO ROAD IS LONG
WITH GOOD COMPANY.

PROVERB

PEOPLE ARE ALWAYS GOOD COMPANY WHEN THEY ARE DOING WHAT THEY REALLY ENJOY.

SAMUEL BUTLER

Somewhere

on the great world

the sun is

always shining,

and it will

sometimes

shine on you.

MYRTLE REED

The sun does not shine for a few trees and flowers, but for the wide world's joy, including yours.

HENRY WARD BEECHER

There is nothing
that cannot happen
today.

MARK   TWAIN

THINK OF A SPECIAL

ORDINARY OCCASION—

THE SUNSET, OR THE

PRESENCE OF ONE YOU

CARE FOR—AND HOW YOU

CAN CELEBRATE IT TODAY.

DAVID KUNDTZ

Slide
down
the banister
every
once in
awhile!

ANONYMOUS

A GOOD LAUGH
IS SUNSHINE IN A HOUSE.

WILLIAM THACKERAY

There is absolutely

no reason for

being rushed along

with the rush.

Everybody should

be free to go slow.

ROBERT FROST

THE RULE IS
JAM TOMORROW
AND JAM YESTERDAY—
BUT NEVER JAM
TODAY.

LEWIS CARROLL

Have a good time, relax, and enjoy. Feel that you want to repeat it. Desire to share it with those who are important to you.

STAN GASSMAN

We wish you sunshine on your path and storms to season your journey. We wish you peace in the world in which you live and in the smallest corner of the heart where truth is kept... More we cannot wish you except perhaps love to make all the rest worthwhile.

ROBERT A. WARD

Success means we go to sleep at night knowing that our talents and abilities were used in a way that served others.

MARIANNE WILLIAMSON

Anyone who
gives a lot
will succeed.
Anyone who
renews others
will be renewed.

PROVERBS 11:25

THE JOY THAT WE GIVE TO OTHERS
IS THE JOY THAT COMES BACK TO US.

JOHN GREENLEAF WHITTIER

Our greatest pleasure is

that which rebounds from hearts

that we've made glad.

HENRY WARD BEECHER

WHEN WE COUNT
OUR BLESSINGS,
WE COUNT YOU
TWICE.

IRISH PROVERB

Special times

and special places.

The moments pass

so quickly.

But the memories

last forever.

UNKNOWN

May your trails be crooked, winding,
lonesome, dangerous, leading to
the most amazing view. May your
mountains rise above the clouds.

EDWARD ABBEY

MAY YOU ALWAYS

FIND NEW ROADS

TO TRAVEL,

NEW HORIZONS

TO EXPLORE,

NEW DREAMS

TO CALL YOUR OWN.

ROBERT BENCHLEY

the good life™

Celebrating the joy of living fully.

Also available are these spirited
companion books in The Good Life
series of great quotations:

drive
friend
heart
hero
joy
moxie
service
spirit
success
thanks
value
vision
yes!